# Football Fun

Written by Simon Mugford

# Football is a good game to play.

# All you need is a ball and some friends!

You can play football in the park.

This park has a football net.
You can play in goal.

You can kick the ball and pass it to your friend.

You can shoot the ball in the net! Goal!

You can play football in a team.

A football team has a coach.

A football team has a kit.

shirt

shorts

shin pads

boots

# You can play in a football match ...

... or you can just play football for fun!

# Talk about the book

Ask your child these questions:

**1** Where can football be played?

**2** What word is used when the ball goes in the net?

**3** Who helped the team learn how to play football?

**4** Name three different pieces of football kit.

**5** Do you like playing football? Why or why not?

**6** What is your favourite game to play with your friends?